you

Building Vehicles that Fly

by Tammy Enz

raintree

91120000361927

Raintree is an imprint of Capstone Global Library Limited, a company incorporated in England and Wales having its registered office at 264 Banbury Road, Oxford OX2 7DY – Registered company number: 6695582

www.raintree.co.uk
myorders@raintree.co.uk

Text © Capstone Global Library Limited 2017
The moral rights of the proprietor have been asserted.

Edited by Adrian Vigliano
Designed by Philippa Jenkins
Picture research by Svetlana Zhurkin
Production by Katy LaVigne
Originated by Capstone Global Library Ltd
Printed and bound in India.

ISBN 978 1 4747 3705 0 (hardback)
21 20 19 18 17
10 9 8 7 6 5 4 3 2 1

ISBN 978 1 4747 3709 8 (paperback)
21 20 19 18 17
10 9 8 7 6 5 4 3 2 1

British Library Cataloguing in Publication Data
A full catalogue record for this book is available from the British Libra

Acknowledgements
We would like to thank the following for permission to reproduce photographs:
Capstone Studio: Karon Dubke, cover, 8, 9, 10, 11, 14, 15, 18, 19, 22, 23, 26, 27; Shutterstock: Andrey Khachatryan, 13, byvalet, 5, iliuta goean, 21, Philip Arno Photography, 25 (bottom), Phillip Rubino, 29, tobkatrina, 7, Vibrant Image Studio, 17

We would like to thank Harold Pratt for his help in the preparation of this book.

Contents

Some words are shown in bold, **like this.** You can find out what they mean by looking in the glossary.

Forces in flight

Soaring the skies is an amazing feat. But whether a huge aeroplane or a tiny bird, all flyers deal with the four forces of flight. **Weight** and **drag** try to pull flyers from the sky or slow them down. But **thrust** and **lift** fight these forces to keep planes and birds aloft.

lift

thrust

drag

weight

Aeroplane designers carefully balance four forces to allow planes to soar in the sky.

Weight

It takes extra force to keep heavier objects in the air. So most aeroplanes are made from the lightest material possible, usually **aluminium**. Aluminium is lightweight but not as strong as some other materials. So sometimes **composite** materials are used. Composite materials are a mixture of two materials. The composite is stronger than either material on its own.

Engineers are always looking for ways to make aeroplanes lighter.

Experiment with weight

In this experiment you can see how extra weight takes extra force to keep aloft.

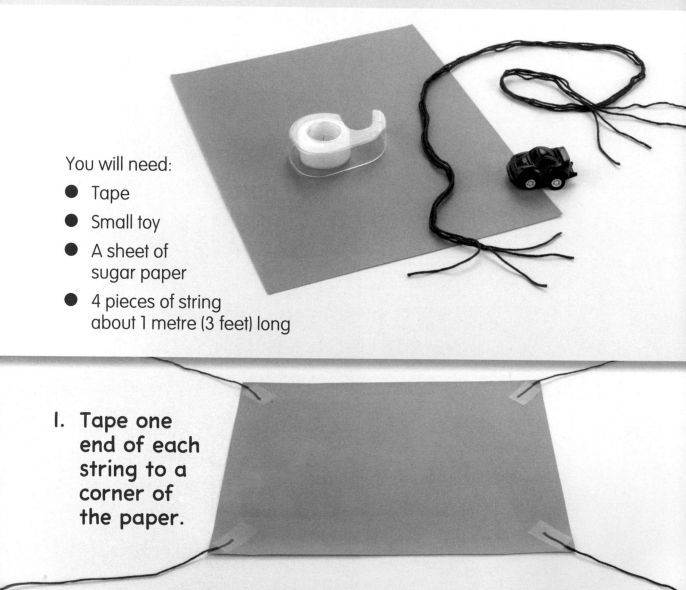

You will need:

- Tape
- Small toy
- A sheet of sugar paper
- 4 pieces of string about 1 metre (3 feet) long

1. Tape one end of each string to a corner of the paper.

2. Tape the other ends of the strings to the top of a door frame. Make sure the paper hangs flat.

3. Blow on the paper from beneath. How hard must you blow to get the paper to rise?

4. Place the toy on the paper.

5. Now how hard must you blow to move the paper?

Experiment with composites

Papier mâché is a composite you can easily make.

You will need:

- Mixing bowl and spoon
- 60 grams (½ cup) flour
- 120 millilitres (½ cup) water
- Paintbrush
- Sheet of plastic
- 20-30 newspaper strips about 3 centimetres (1 inch) wide x 15 cm (6 in) long

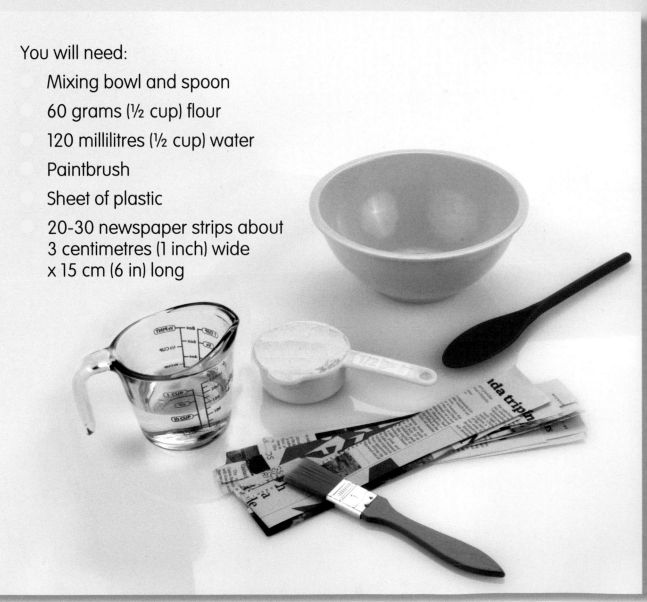

1. Stir the flour and water together in the bowl until smooth.
2. Paint a thin layer of plaster on the sheet of plastic.
3. Lay 5 newspaper strips side by side on the plaster. Paint on another layer of plaster.
4. Lay 5 more strips crosswise on top.
5. Repeat with another layer.
6. Paint a thick layer of plaster on another spot on the plastic.
7. Allow to dry overnight.
8. Peel off the papier mâché and plaster.
9. Now compare a fresh newspaper strip, the dried plaster and the dried papier mâché. Test the materials to see which is strongest.

Drag

As flyers try to push through the air, drag slows them down. Drag is air's push against something as it moves. The faster an object moves, the more drag slows it down. You feel drag when you run very fast. A plane's shape can help lessen drag. Round and tapered surfaces help air move past the plane to reduce drag.

Engineers make planes as smooth as possible to lessen drag.

Experiment with drag

See how an aeroplane's shape affects drag in this experiment.

You will need:

- 2 sheets of paper
- Ruler
- Scissors
- 2 paper clips

1. Crease one piece of paper in half lengthways.

2. Open it and fold the top corners into the crease. Fold the corners in again.

3. Fold the paper in half along the crease.

4. Fold each flap down to make wings.

5. Repeat steps 1-4 with the other piece of paper to make another plane.

6. Measure and cut 3 cm (1 in) off the nose of one plane to make its front blunt.

7. Attach a paper clip to the nose of each plane. Test your planes by flying them. Try to launch the planes identically. Which flies better?

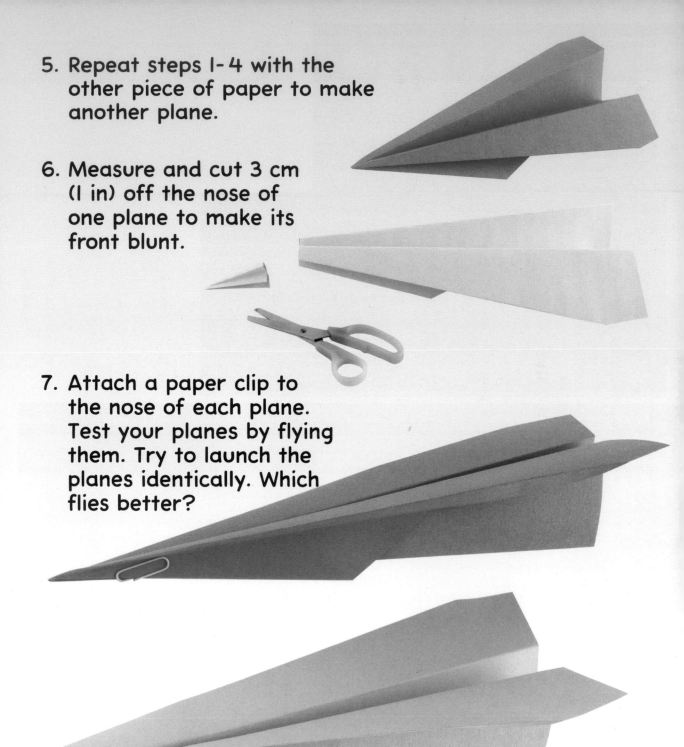

Some flyers count on drag to help them. **Parachutes** help skydivers to move slowly through the air. The parachutes spread out to capture air and increase drag. If you jump from a plane without a parachute you fall to the ground at over 200 kilometres (125 miles) per hour. With a parachute you fall at only about 19 km (12 miles) per hour.

With a parachute, drag can save your life!

Make a parachute

Test out drag by building your own parachute.

You will need:

- A small plastic toy
- 4 pieces of thread 46 cm- (18 in-) long
- A 46 cm (18 in) square of plastic cut from a bin bag

1. Lightly toss the toy into the air. How quickly does it fall?

2. Tie one end of each thread around a corner of the plastic.

3. Tie the other ends of the threads to the toy.

4. Gather the plastic and toy in your hand and toss lightly into the air. Does the parachute help the toy land more slowly?

Thrust

Planes and birds create thrust to fight against weight and drag. Thrust is the force that moves these flyers forward. Birds flap their wings to create thrust. Planes use burning gases to thrust them forward. As gases push out of the back of the plane, the plane moves forward.

Everything that flies must create thrust to stay in the air.

Lift

Thrust moves planes forward. But lift keeps planes aloft. An aeroplane's wings are specially shaped to create lift. Their tapered shape is called an **aerofoil**. As a plane thrusts forward, aerofoil-shaped wings change the air's direction and lift a plane up. Bird's wings are aerofoils too.

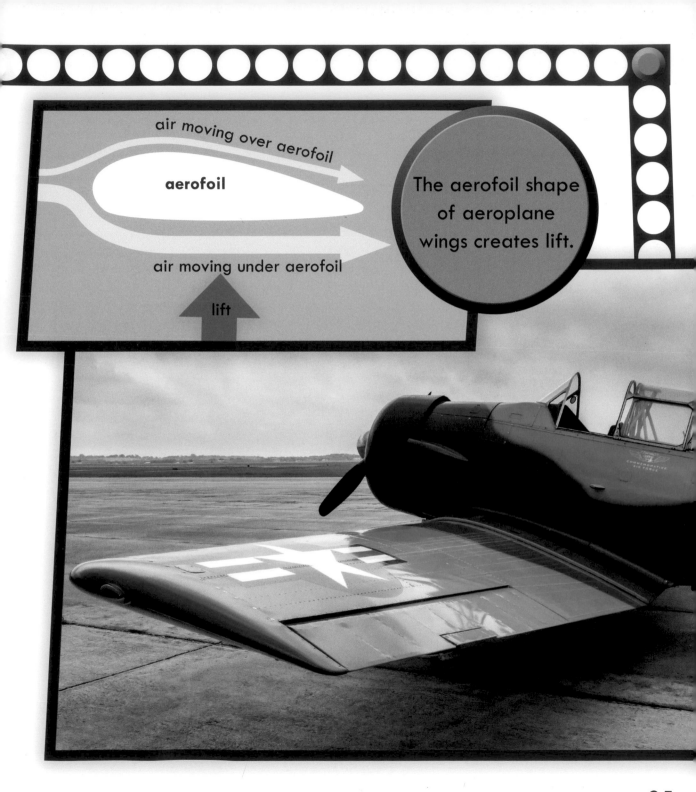

air moving over aerofoil

aerofoil

air moving under aerofoil

lift

The aerofoil shape of aeroplane wings creates lift.

Experiment with aerofoils

Try this experiment to see an aerofoil in action.

You will need:

- A 15-cm (6-in) square piece of sugar paper
- Tape

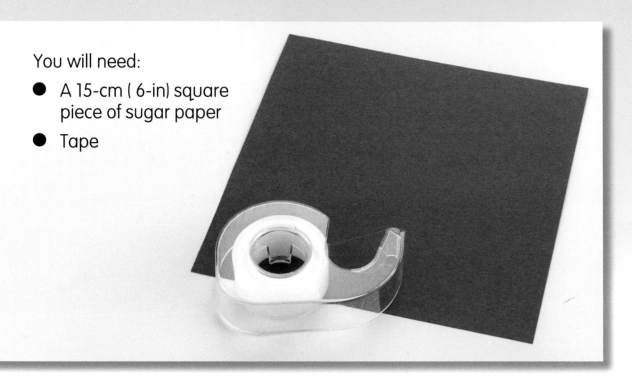

1. Bend the paper so that two edges are touching. Leave the folded edge rounded. Tape the edges together.

2. Place the aerofoil on a table. Hold your hands behind it to prevent it from blowing away.

3. Gently blow directly at the taped edge. Does anything happen?

4. Now flip the aerofoil. Blow at the rounded edge. Now does the aerofoil lift? Try flattening the bottom of your aerofoil then blowing on the rounded edge again. Does this change how it moves?

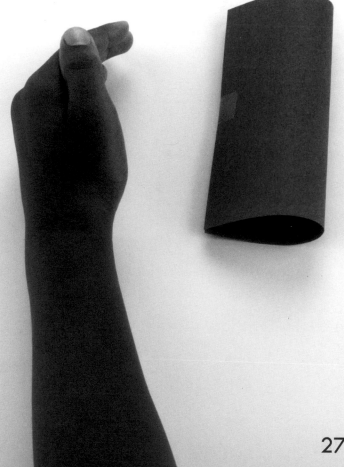

Flight seems baffling. But it is less so when you understand the forces of flight. Think about these forces the next time you see a plane take off or a bird fly by. Know that they stay aloft by balancing the forces of flight: weight, drag, lift and thrust.

Engineers work hard each day to design the next great aeroplane.

Glossary

aerofoil rounded wing that creates lift

aluminium light metal

composite material made from two different materials

drag slowing force from air

lift rising force caused by a moving aerofoil

parachute cloth that fills with air to slow a falling object

thrust pushing force

weight heaviness of something

Find out more

Books

Aircraft (How to Build), Rita Storey (Franklin Watts, 2016)

Planes (What's Inside), David West (Franklin Watts, 2016)

Superplanes (Mean Machines), Paul Harrison (Franklin Watts, 2014)

Websites

www.dkfindout.com/uk/transport/history-aircraft

Learn about the history of aircraft on the DK Find Out website.

www.funkidslive.com/learn/amys-aviation

Find out everything you need to know about aviation on the Fun Kids website.

www.nms.ac.uk/explore/games/plane-builder/

Build your own plane for a jungle rescue in this game from National Museums Scotland

Index